Hi, this is Charles Smith Author of Footprints and the Life Long Experience books. One way you can help any author is by leaving a review on Amazon.com, I would really appreciate an honest review about what you thought of this book. ☐

All content copyright © CHARLES SMITH 2022

ALL RIGHTS RESERVED

No part of this book may be reproduced in any form or by any electronic or mechanical means including information storage and retrieval systems, without permission in writing from the author. The only exception is by a reviewer, who may quote short excerpts in a review.

FOOTPRINTS is presented for informational purposes only. Charles Smith is not responsible for any injuries that may occur mentally or physically when doing anything presented in this book. It is best to consult a doctor before doing anything that may be stressful for your mind or body. I Charles Smith am also not responsible for anything triggering in this book. Please use your best judgment while reading this book and consult a therapist before answering the questions in this book that you think may be triggering!

CONTENTS

My Grandfather was one of the greatest men I have ever known; I never got a chance to tell him, though. When my father died to the day my grandfather died (a 17-year span), I was caught in my own downward spiral. I thought the world owed me for being orphaned. My mother died when I was six, and my father died when I was eleven.

I never let anyone into my heart, especially family. I could not accept that my parents passed away, and damn anyone who tried to take their place. That was my thinking back then. I had friends sure that I consider brothers to this day; back then, they were the only positive coping skill I let in.

The day my grandfather passed away, I knelt by his hospital bed and swore to him I would make him proud of me one day. The rush of emotions I felt that day was a mixture of anger, guilt, sadness, and shame. I was angry at myself, ashamed and guilty that I never told him how I felt until now. Of course, the sadness was because our family just lost our greatest rock in the family, the world lost a beloved man, and the heavens gained one of its greatest angels!

That day was just the beginning of some of the darkest days of my life. Shortly after that, my uncle, who raised me, passed away, and after that, I fell into my deepest depression. I became a carver, cutting on myself to feel something other than the pain I felt. I was empty, all I felt in my soul was pain, and I eventually attempted suicide. After my failed attempt, I ended up homeless and bouncing from veteran's shelter to veteran's shelter for a little more than five years until I got myself back on my feet. These years would be known as my crucible, and I became the better person for surviving it.

At times, my family jokes in a not so funny way that we lost more people than the Kennedys. In my 50 years, from my parents when I was young to my cousin that I idolized growing up, my uncle that raised me, to one of my best friends in life, John Ellis, too many friends and family members; I lost over twenty close people in all.

That is what this book is about, accepting the loss you are suffering from, Facing the levels of grief you are feeling, and letting your pain out. Gaining coping skills and letting go of regrets. Being around friends and family who care.

In every book I write, I combine life experience and research I've done on the subject, Footprints is no different. In the research that I have done for this book, I looked at the 5-7 stages of grief, denial, guilt, anger, bargaining, depression, awakening (upward turn), reconstruction of your life, and acceptance. I began to think about them all, this is what Footsteps focuses upon. Talking about each one and how to get from the shock of stage one (denial) to the seventh stage (acceptance).

Keep in mind though that these do not go in order, for instance with one of the most profound deaths in my life, my uncle; I began bargaining before the actual death took place. This can often happen when someone has a disease like cancer, or life-threatening injuries. Anger can be the same, and so can depression. My point is though, they do not go in the order I will be discussing them in this book. Just like coping skills, it is different for everyone. Then we will focus on some coping skills that can support you while going through these stages and trying to move on with your life.

No part of this book may be reproduced in any form or by any electronic or mechanical means including information storage and retrieval systems, without permission in writing from the author. The only exception is by a reviewer, who may quote short excerpts in a review.

FOOTPRINTS is presented for informational purposes only. Charles Smith is not responsible for any injuries that may occur mentally or physically when doing anything presented in this book. It is best to consult a doctor before doing anything that may be stressful for your mind or body. I Charles Smith am also not responsible for anything triggering in this book. Please use your best judgment while reading this book and consult a therapist before answering the questions in this book that you think may be triggering!

DEDICATION

This book is dedicated to my Mother Barbra Smith, Father Lyle Smith, Grandfather Joseph Direnzo, Grandmother Margaret Direnzo, Uncle Vincent Buffone, his parents Mary & Lee Buffone, Aunt Judy Greene, Cousin Ricky Direnzo, and lifelong friend John Ellis, and the others both friends and family I have lost in my life. I say lost, but keep in mind that if you keep them in your heart, they are never truly gone.

I also dedicate this book to you, the reader who has lost a loved one. May you find acceptance in your heart and discover a way of healing in this new normal you find yourself in.

WHEN YOU SEE A CLOUD,
IT'S TIME TO THINK ABOUT
WHAT YOU JUST READ.

GET YOUR JOURNALS READY!

I'm often asked where I got this picture, and are the footprints real? This is a picture taken by my sister of the family's house on a lake in Massachusetts, we call it The Camp. The footprints are in fact real, and the reason I chose this, for this book's cover. The footprints are of unknown origin, we're not sure who's they are. To me it represents everyone who has come and gone from The Camp, and family members who are no longer with us.

When I asked the artist Hermes to do an illustration of the picture for the book, I was blown away, he captured it perfectly!!

Thank you, Hermes, and my sister Christina! ☐

WHAT ARE COPING SKILLS?

The first topic I need to discuss here is coping skills, so we are all on the same page per say. Coping skills are what we do to support our wellbeing, we use them to motivate ourselves, and to feel better about ourselves with confidence in our hearts.

There are positive and negative coping skills, for some unforeseen reason we are more easily drawn to the negative ones when we are feeling depressed or overwhelmed. Negative coping skills can include drug or alcohol abuse, and abuse of other types like fighting (domestic abuse) and bullying. This may also include self-harm, blaming yourself, all or nothing thinking, withdrawing from friends, excessive gambling, just to name a few.

Positive coping skills include things as simple as breathing, a few slow deep breaths, or breathing in for 7 seconds, out for 11 seconds a few times. Saying "no" to something negative in your life and having people around that you trust and that will have a positive influence in your life. Punching a punching bag, laughing, eating healthy and going on nature hikes.

In these next sections you will be thinking about what you will be using as positive coping skills to get you through the challenging times you may be facing, why you picked up this book. I have guided 100's of people in finding their own coping skills, now it's your turn. The tricky thing though, you must find your own, I can tell you what works for me like writing, breathing techniques, or martial arts, and guide you in the right direction, but the choice is yours. I can lead you to the water, but you must choose to drink it.

WHAT ARE SOME COPING SKILLS
YOU THINK WOULD WORK FOR YOU
TO LIVE A HAPPIER LIFE?

Imagine, it's back in June 2021 and the world around us is in turmoil. Covid-19 is still running ragged although the numbers have gone down around us; new variants are popping up all around us like the new Mexican variant and the delta variant. We will never hit herd immunity because not enough people trust our government and its vaccines.

Now, on top of this, gun violence is in an all-time high with mass shootings happening daily. Just last weekend there was four mass shootings in 6 hours leaving thirty-nine wounded, and five dead. On top of that, most states are removing federal unemployment stimulus. When 1,000s of people claim next week they will get a much smaller check to support their families. In a couple of months if not sooner, the homeless rate will go up, even if half the people unemployed do find jobs!

Then there is us, the people on the bottom of this huge pile and our mental health status are at an all-time low. A lot of people never experienced this type of hardship. I remember talking with a friend back then, she said I don't seem effected by it, and is that because of everything I've experienced in life? I replied to her kiddingly "yeah, I'm used to chaos" but in all honesty I've been affected by it also, I notice my mood dropping some, but then I take the necessary steps to recoup. This is where coping skills are paramount, I explained to her!

Positive coping skills ease the suffering we face, in a positive way. It makes it more tolerable to get up in the morning and face the day. Coping skills encompass your life, eating healthier, getting a good night's sleep, being around good influential people, things that release tension without negative side effects, like my eight-year-old son says, "make good choices."

Coping skills keep you from "burnout," burnout is when you get so tired, you just do not care about anything and you feel detached, alone in the world. You begin to feel overwhelmed with a negative outlook, doubting yourself. A prime example of this is a story I heard from a professor once. He knew a police officer that was on a terrible car wreck scene. In one of the cars was a child, and this child was bleeding. When he got the child out of the vehicle, he got blood on his uniform. This officer was more concerned about the blood on his uniform than the child's condition. This is a severe case of burnout, and the officer requested leave after that day knowing something wasn't right with his reaction to the accident.

MOVING FORWARD

When my father died, I was eleven years old. I did not talk for 6 months from the shock my sister tells me. I hardly remember coming back to Massachusetts because we were in Van Horn Texas when he passed away. We were now orphans living under our aunt and uncle's roof and our grandparents would be our guardians. I remember wanting no part of it and making that abundantly clear in my own way. I always tell people they could give me anything and it would not have mattered, I could not have the two things I wanted, my parents back.

For many years I was "stuck" in a fog of unmanageable depression unable to move forward with my life and felt all the symptoms of PTSD when it was known as battle fatigue. All I felt was numbness, feeling lost in my own skin, very keyed up. I acted out constantly and found myself grounded, or in the principal's office/guidance counselor's office often. Every time I tried to move forward it was in the wrong direction and/or two steps backward.

That is how a lot of us are, I think, when we lose a loved one, especially one as significant as a parent as a young child, not knowing how to process. When you are a child, they say you may be too young to understand, I think when we do not utterly understand we tend to turn inward and shut down, afraid of the reality we must inevitably face. How do we understand death though, even as an adult? I have lost many like my uncle who raised me, and my cousin, both died too young, and trying to make sense of that is just not something I could do. Moving forward from loss and attempting to live a new life with pieces taken out is not easy. It's like putting together a 100-piece puzzle with one piece now gone, no matter how many times you attempt to build it, it's not the same.

These can include just getting up in the morning and not staying in bed all day. Depression can be like the great wall of China sitting on your chest when you are trying to move forward after dealing with something like a death and loss.

You must fight it with reverse psychology, if you want to stay in bed, get up. If you do not want to exercise, go to the gym. If you do not want to eat, think of a meal you really enjoy and make or order it. It is proven that you get more out of things you want to do, but you are lacking the motivation to do them. You end up feeling more satisfaction and enjoyment in them.

LET'S CONSIDER SOME POSITIVE
COPING SKILLS TO SUPPORT YOU IN
MOVING FORWARD NOW!

Sometimes even if we cannot understand it, we must accept it to move forward in life. It is true what they say, "nothing hit's harder than life" except for death.

I can remember just a few years ago, my aunt was diagnosed with cancer, I felt like I stared death in the eyes, and I blinked with my head bowed, I cringed and coward like a little kid seeing the monster in the closet! I thought, how is this possible???

I was just swimming with her the summer before at our family lake house, the same lake pictured on the cover, and she was fine or so it seemed! She is the one who called my son and I every night on our Florida/Lego Land trip last year. I was so scared of losing her and afraid of breaking down as I did almost twenty years ago now when my uncle and Grandfather died a month apart. This time around I have some excellent coping skills in place but still, it scared me more than ever now. It scared me so much I made excuses to not see her at first, and that may sound unforgiving, but it was self-preservation to me, and the fear had me paralyzed.

After she died, it was a harsh reality slap, to say the least! I kept thinking to myself, I am the one in the family that should have been there. Because of my skills in human services, I should have been there. It was my PTSD and my strongest trigger (death) that left me powerless, and I thought if I see her, I would be a wreck. I did end up seeing her a couple times towards the end of her life, and I was there with the rest of my family the day she passed, but I will always regret not being there more, which is why I decided to author this book on this subject; for me as much for you.

Another more recent passing was when my lifelong friend John passed away. He had been battling cancer for almost a decade. A couple of his old friends and I went up north to see him, and the reality slap was seeing him in person. The cancer had aged him to the appearance of an 80yr old man. He was still John on the inside, his demeanor was like he was last time we seen him. We all joked if he died on us while we were out, we were going to do what they did in the movie Weekend at Bernie's lol.

Laughter was our way of coping, usually has been. The following week, we heard little from him, and the weekend after that, he had passed away. At least we had one more weekend with him, our old friend. Now though, no one was laughing, accepting the reality slap was hard even though we knew it was coming. We all go through that at times, I think. We know something unthinkable is about to happen, but when it happens it still hits us hard…

When I think of this one, I think of the one thing that changed my life, see, most of my life I regrated being left alone. My parents leaving me here. What I know now is what I did not know back then and that is that they did not leave me alone, they never left me. I will mention this a couple times in this book, but if you keep the ones who passed on in your heart, and live for their memory, then they are never truly gone.

Once I realized this, it was so enlightening, and man did I need that at that time! I accepted my life, and their death, living for their memory and how they would want me to live. I live a fulfilling life, not depressed, and missing them. I talk to them when I need to, and If I close my eyes and think of them, I can see them.

SITTING WITH THE PAIN, FACING IT.

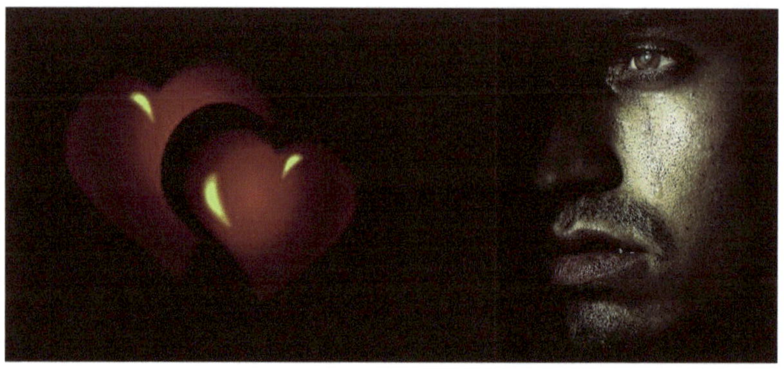

This is the hardest thing for any of us. Facing this kind of pain that cuts so deep into your heart that you will do anything to stop it, and a lot of us like myself, unfortunately, used negative coping skills like drugs or carving ourselves, or even suicide attempts to numb that pain. We can even go on for years hating people who try to get close to us, for the simple reason, they try to get close to us. We are afraid to let anyone in because if we do, we might lose them too.

When my father died, I was with him in a hospital near Van Horn Texas. He opened his eyes for a moment, looked at me, held my hand, the next second, he was gone. For years after that, I was just so angry, that he left us. In the years to follow until 2001 when my uncle and Grandfather died, I acted out, angry, doing anything I could to numb the pain and to get negative attention. The positive attention did not matter to me really. Then when my uncle and Grandfather died, well, regret seems like such an understatement, but I regrated how I was all those years, never letting them know how I felt, how thankful I was for taking care of us all those years.

What I did not realize back then is something that I tell people all the time now, is what I just said; but worth repeating. If we live for their memories, keep them in our hearts and live the way they would want us to live, in our own way then they are never truly gone. That is the secret of dealing with the loss of loved ones, as painful as it is. It is sitting with the pain, facing that pain, and turning it into something good. It is celebrating their life, not mourning their death or your loss, at least not to the extent of it taking over your life. Make them proud of you, because they are up there watching you, and the only way they can rest, is if you get that pain out.

Now, with that being said; it is not all a bed of roses. We will still mourn; we will still get angry and very emotional; it is a human reaction to death and loss. I remember when my cousin died of an overdose, it took all I had to not go and take my anger out on every drug dealer I met, with my background I could have created such a crap-storm!

I remember meeting a drug dealer in one of the rehabs I worked at, he was a big-time dealer too. I had thoughts of pushing him down a flight of stairs once or twice or working late and having myself a blanket party, things that would not come back on me, "oh he must have tripped", or "I have no clue what happened, I was in my office doing paperwork"; I did not though, instead I got to know him, told him my story, and he deeply regrated dealing after meeting me and seeing the others in rehab that he probably put there. He told me a lot about the drug-dealing world that I did not know, and instead of taking my anger out on him and others like him, I learned about the world that took my cousin away and met some incredibly good-hearted people along the way. I eventually told him, I am glad I never killed him, in a jokingly way.

COPING SKILLS FOR SITTING WITH THE PAIN, FACING IT

Well, first off, do not use a negative coping skill like finding every drug dealer you can and beating them to death, or getting drugs from those dealers. Though I do not drink now, I know a lot of people who have a drink or two a day, just do not do it in excess especially to sooth the pain. Instead use the lesson on the last page and live for their memory, honor their life. How you do it is the part of this coping skill you have to figure out for yourself.

WHAT CAN YOU DO TO
HONOR THEIR LIFE?

One reason I write, is for myself, it is filling a void that feels like that vastness of space at times and trying to make some sense of all the things I have been through. After someone dies, we often feel empty inside. We may have a flood of emotions overtake us like sadness, or anger but, we still have that empty void that our loved ones once filled. This is where living for their memory can become vital.

Like a black hole of negativity that void can grow and swallow you up like a black hole will swallow up a planet if we allow it to do so! We need to fill that space with positivity instead of negativity, which is the only way we can begin to heal. Healing ourselves is what they want. No one that you ever loved, and they loved you back would want you to be depressed, angry, or hurting in any way.

Believe me when I say I know all of this is easier said than done. I can tell you though the difference between being stuck in that pain for decades, and releasing the pain, or redirecting the energy that pain takes up, into something positive and worthwhile is very uplifting and rewarding. My question for you is, how do you want to live with this loss? Lying in bed wallowing in pity or getting up and making something positively amazing to honor them like a book, song, poem, non-profit…the list can go on and on how to fill this void.

COPING SKILLS TO FILL THAT VOID

One thing you can do is continue traditions you loved to do with your loved one like making Christmas cookies, or coloring Easter eggs with remaining members of the family, or group of friends. You can also, like I said, do something to honor their memory like a poem, book, song, or create a non-profit in their memory, sharing their love with others. Know that no one can fill that void, but it will allow you to feel a little less empty inside. Another thing you can do is mend any broken pieces of your heart with worthwhile people in your life and try new hobbies with friends. Stay busy and keep the mind focused on the here and now.

WHAT ARE SOME IDEAS
TO FILL THAT VOID?
THEY CAN BE SHORT TERM LIKE A
MOVIE OR COOKIES, OR LONG TERM
LIKE WRITING A BOOK.

Looking for a new normal seems to be the norm these days 2020/21. Sometimes though we go through this on less of a global scale and we feel alone, which is the reason it says "You Are Not Alone" on the front cover. It is important to know you are not alone as you discover a new life without your loved one next to you. Remember though they are never too far away, they are in your heart.

I told you about my aunt that passed away just before Christmas of 2019. A new normal for me was the summer after, as my family went down to our lake house, we call the Camp. The summer after was a lot different without her there, it did not feel anything like it did. I ended up only going down there because my son wanted us to go down so he could play with his cousins. It still did not feel like it did, there was just an emptiness to it.

How do we find a new normal after a tragic loss? All death is tragic do not get me wrong, but an unexpected death like an accident, overdose or suicide can feel more tragic because it is suddenly and shockingly ripping your world apart. When someone dies of old age, or a death from a longer lasting illness, you have time to prepare for it. Either way though, you are looking at discovering a new normal after they pass on.

The first death I experienced was like that, when I was six and my mother died of an overdose it drastically changed my world. I have that story in my book 10 Homes in 11 Years, the name of that book though just barely begins to describe the changes in my life after that.

I went on to Facebook last night and a friend posted that his son just committed suicide earlier that day, my heart sank. I did not know his son, but being a suicide survivor myself I was automatically brought back to that time, and thought "what makes me any different than his son, why did I survive?" Questions like that will never be answered, just like why someone felt the need to end their life in that way. Questions like that can leave an emptiness in you that may never be filled, except with grief.

COPING SKILLS FOR DISCOVERING
A NEW NORMAL

Just looking at the couple years of COVID, we have all had to discover a new normal, well most of us anyway. We had to social distance from the ones we love, wear masks, work from home, or find other jobs. Some of us lost our homes, loved ones, jobs, and our new normal seems like a nightmare we cannot wake from.

First and most importantly, we must not push ourselves to find a new normal. If we push ourselves, we can become overwhelmed quickly and get discouraged, in this very emotional time. Create a new routine, staying on the old one as much as possible. Limit yourself at first to "reminders" as much as possible. Your heart and mind will not heal if you are surrounded by reminders of the loss. This is not by any means telling you to forget about your loved one, it is just giving you some healing space and time. In fact, I will say this repeatedly throughout this book but, keeping them close to your heart after you have a good sense of healing is one of the best coping strategies I can suggest.

ENVISION A NEW NORMAL.
WHAT DOES IT LOOK LIKE?
BE IMAGINATIVE AND PUT IN AS
MUCH DETAIL AS POSSIBLE.

The stages do not have to go in order. For instance, before my Uncle Vinny died, we knew he was extremely sick with cancer. I found myself bargaining for his life with God, asking him to take me instead. I was deeply depressed at the time after my grandfather passed and felt my uncle had more to offer the world. The way I seen it, he had a family, children, so much to live for; I was the exact opposite. At that point of my life, I just felt like I was existing, and would have gladly traded places. Sometimes, no matter what hand you have, you cannot change the inevitable.

When someone you love gets sick with cancer, or has a life-threatening injury, you just feel helpless, it is out of your hands. You begin to pray to whoever will listen up there and do things you would not normally do.

The "what ifs" and the "if I only did this or that" come into your head. If I had called him or her, before they got into their car, I could have offered a ride and they would not have crashed. Then there is the if I went to the hospital to see him or her, I could have said goodbye before they passed away, that was me the night before my uncle passed away. I worked a long shift at work that day and felt if I got some rest, I would be refreshed and see him the next day, sometimes we do not get that next day.

The truth to the matter is, a lot of us do have regrets when it comes to death, we could have done this or that at this time or that place. If we hold onto those instead of the blessings of memories, we just feed the depression that is currently growing inside of us.

COPING SKILLS FOR BARGAINING

This is a tricky one to talk about, and it is all in your own point of view. A lot of people will "bargain" or use prayer to ask their higher power for healing. You tell them that you will do anything if they can heal your loved one, even healing you from the grief you feel. If you do not get what you want from that, you may get angry at yourself, the situation, or higher power. The best coping skills for this are to write down what you want, and more importantly, why?

For instance, years back a friend of mine wanted me to pray for his brother's recovery after he was in an accident. I told him, I would light a candle, and meditate, sending positive energy that things turn out the best for his brother. His brother was a regularly active person, and happy go lucky. My friend wanted his brother to live on, as any brother would, but if his brother did live on, he would have been in a vegetative state for the rest of his life. What is the best for him? It is not up to me, or anyone else to say.

He ended up passing away a month after, and sometime after that my friend told me that even though he misses his brother; he thinks his brother is in a better place, and everything did turn out best in the situation. On the next page write down what you want, and more importantly, why?

WHAT DO YOU WANT?
MORE IMPORTANTLY, WHY DO YOU WANT IT?

THINK THIS THROUGH

WHAT IS THE BEST SOLUTION TO CREATE
THE BEST OUTCOME FOR EVERYONE?

GROWING FROM THE LOSS

Carrying on after the loss of a loved one can make you feel alone and helpless. It is extremely difficult to work through and reconstruct your life, but it can be done. Putting the pieces of your life back together after dealing with loss is like that puzzle, I mentioned with one piece missing, you can either stare at that one piece that's missing until it becomes a blackhole, or you can learn to see the beauty of the entire picture. It is not easy at all, but you can do it, and you will continue.

You must take time to mourn, I mentioned this before with my aunt's death, but it was like death stared me in the face and I blinked for the first time in my life. No other death in my family affected me like this. I felt anger when my cousin died, I felt loss and deep depression when my uncle and Grandfather died, but never this feeling of "mortality" like when my aunt died. It took me weeks and a good talk with my Sensi to begin to feel like myself again.

I was reminded of her last summer, and I think of her every day, like I did the others I lost in my life. I keep her in my heart and live for her memory. I grow knowing she loved me and remember the good times we shared, instead of how I was growing up, not letting anyone in, hating life, and doing whatever I can to forget, if just for that moment. When we do this, we wake up and feel like utter crap, with nothing changed in our lives.

Like I have said throughout this book, holding them in my heart and living for their memory is a positive way to grow after a loss, but how do you, yourself do it? Coping skills for growing after a loss are just like every other coping skill, it must be your own. Taking the time to mourn, remember them, and continuing what they loved in life. Find your way to support their memory…

HOW WILL YOU REMEMBER THEM
AND CONTINUE WHAT THEY LOVED IN LIFE?
FIND YOUR WAY TO SUPPORT THEIR MEMORY...

In this section I want to talk about something that plagued me for most of my life, negative thoughts. When I became orphaned, I became terribly angry, negative thoughts would reign in my brain for decades, I would dwell on everything that went wrong in my life, and I hated the fact that my parents left me here.

It is safe to say a lot of us go through this negative thinking pattern when we lose someone we love. Some of us even get swallowed up by this vortex of negativity and self-pity and lose all interest in life. Lying in bed and watching life just pass them by.

How do we change those thoughts from negative to positive? Well, like I was saying in previous sections, there are many ways to honor our loved ones when they pass on, and honoring their life is one of the best ways we can turn our thinking around. Help them to live on, and mourn the loss, but celebrate the life. I remember a Disney movie my son and I watched called Coco about a child named Miguel who loved music but was forbidden to play by his family who put a ban on music for the entire clan.

When Miguel strummed a late musician's guitar and was transported to another plane of existence, he met his Great Grandfather during the Day of The Dead Festival. His Grandfather was afraid of being forgotten on our plane of existence because he would fade away on the other side. It was the child's mission in the movie to support him in living on in the family's memory, so he is not forgotten. In doing so, the child's spirits were lifted because his grandfather turned out to be the one who wrote music for the musician who owned the guitar, and in doing what Miguel did he lifted the music ban, and he was able to play. It is the same for us, doing what we can to sustain the memory of our loved ones will in turn lift our spirits, and that is what it is all about.

COPING SKILLS FOR LIFTING OUR SPIRITS

First off, let it out, if you are a woman or a man, young or old, it is ok to cry. Crying is a perfectly natural emotional response. Letting emotions build up inside you is only going to cause more pain. Loss of a loved one is one of the toughest things you can experience in life, as I said earlier nothing hits harder than life, except death.

With that all being said, what can you do to lift your spirits? This is all on you, if it is going bowling, or playing pool, or just a joy ride in the country, or watching a good comedy. Whatever you do for fun, and to get your mind better in tune with the here and now and in a more positive mood.

On the next page, I want you to make a list of fun things to do. I recommend some of these things be done with family or friends. Remember there is a difference between being alone and being lonely, after a loss like this, we are often lonely, so be around people you love. This reminds me of a movie I have seen once that is a fitting example. The main character fulfilled his loved one's dream of going on a cruise and bringing their ashes with him. Along the way on the cruise, he scattered his loved one's ashes in the ocean. That stuck with me because I thought it was such a loving gesture. So now it is your turn, not for a cruise unless that is what you want to do, but just go out and enjoy yourself…

WHAT ARE SOME IDEAS FOR
LIFTING YOUR SPIRITS?
IT'S A TIME FOR MOURNING,
BUT ALSO, A TIME TO HONOR THEIR LIVES.

Are any of us emotionally stable after the last couple years (2020-2022) we just went through??? This reminds me of an episode of the Arrow, it was when Oliver (Arrow) was told by his friend that he was fine after a tragic event, and Oliver told him he would be worried if he thought that was true.

On any given year though, often after a loss, or other tragic event we might look fine on the outside, but on the inside, we are an emotional mess. No matter what we do to mask our feelings they eventually become known at the surface. One of the ways we accept loss and move forward from loss is to truly heal on the inside.

This is where acceptance really come in, as difficult as it is at the time. We will never get over loss, but we can accept it in time, and learn new ways to move forward in our own lives. Just like the tagline for my book series "don't just cover up our wounds, heal from within." It is often harder than healing a wound, because it does not take a band-aid, it takes heart, willpower, and focus to truly heal from within and become emotionally stable.

COPING SKILLS FOR STAYING EMOTIONALLY STABLE

Luckily, there is not a lack of coping skills for staying emotionally stable. It is harder getting to the action phase of coping skills when we are not emotionally stable. Like I say throughout this book, I can tell you about good coping skills, but it is all on your which ones will work for you. Have fun with it though, get out and try new things, laugh, love, and live.

Go out and get your nails done, or for us guys, go shoot some pool with the guys, although I admit, I had a gothic phase where I wore black or blood red nail polish. Any-hoot, this is about coping skills, not my life phases.

Go out for a nature walk, look at pictures of fun times you spent with your loved ones, take a nice bath, find a new hobby. The list can go on and on like listening to music, using aromatherapy, or drawing even if you're me and cannot draw a stick figure…

WHAT WOULD IT TAKE
TO MAKE YOU FEEL EMOTIONALLY STABLE?
FAVORITE FOOD? MOVIE?
RIDE IN THE COUNTRYSIDE?
THIS IS A MARATHON OF MANY STEPS...

This is one thing that often comes up when people are dealing with loss. We look for someone to blame and when we do not find someone we start looking above, to our higher power. The problem is we are looking to blame and not for comfort, salvation, or enlightenment. I have gone through it myself, for a lot of my life I denounced my faith in Christianity because of the loss of my parents. I have researched every other religion and found that I believe in them all, even Jediism, yes, that is an actual religion based off the Star Wars Jedi.

Who am I to say one or another does not exist? I tell people a lot in my programs that if someone worshiped a doorknob and that got them through the day, I would not tell them it is wrong, because it got them through the day and it gives them strength, encouragement, and something to believe in, I do not belong to any religion myself, my faith is in humanity and the universe.

How do we retain our faith when it is in question though? Evaluating our faith when something so tragic as a loss of a loved one can be extremely difficult. I look at it this way, whichever God you worship gave you that annoying free will, and some deaths are caused by free will. Take the person who smoked cigarettes for 50 years and then died of cancer, it was their free will to smoke. Or that person in the military who died of a gunshot wound, it was their free will to join up.

It is not gods fault, and that is the first time I said that aloud, but it is not. Even when something tragic happens to a child, like the mass shooting in Orange County California a few days ago where a child was one of the victims. We may question where God was, why he did not protect them, and this is where it gets tricky even to write this section. I heard once though that God may have taken them to spare them from something in the future, I am not sure what I believe about this, but it is better than believing any God or Goddess was absent that day and did nothing. In the end evaluation of your faith is your choice, and that is your free will.

COPING SKILLS
FOR EVALUATING YOUR FAITH.

One of the first things we need to think of is, things happen, and sometimes there is no reasoning that we will ever understand, or even know. We go through anger and blaming as part of the healing process at times, but we can move on from this. This is done by allowing happiness back into your life, as time allows. This is an uphill battle just as it is with any depression, and it seems the closer the person was to you, the steeper the hill. Evaluating your faith is up to you, right now may be too soon.

When my uncle and Grandfather died, I had no higher power, until I became homeless. I was in a Veteran's shelter and met a man who introduced me to the Wiccan religion. I felt like my faith in Christianity was never going to be restored. This new faith restored that part of my life and began a path of researching different religions and eventually restoring my faith in God and Jesus and all the above, because as I mentioned it is all real and I am no one to say otherwise.

WHAT CAN BE DONE TO
REESTABLISH YOUR FAITH,
AND BRING PEACE BACK INTO YOUR LIFE?

Mindfulness is being in the here and now, focused on what is present in your life without judgment. When it comes to loss it involves opening to the loss, not fighting the acceptance of it, but letting it in fully and completely becoming one with the loss. When you do this, you end up with a "new normal" that is different, but one you can tolerate and even be ok with.

I was doing a guided meditation on change in life this morning, well, softening resistance to change that is, and there is no bigger change than losing a loved one in someone's life. We can soften the resistance through acceptance and mindfulness. It must be a gentle process; it cannot be rushed. I believe we must feel the emotions that come with the good, bad, and the ugliness of life.

The trick is to feel it without delay, and go forward, not to dwell on it. I know people who have sat with their pain for decades and it has destroyed them, do not let that be you.

COPING SKILLS THAT BRING MINDFULNESS TO LIFE

I was sitting in on my acupuncture appointment the other day. For a half hour, I had to sit leaned back in a chair, needles in my head, hands, and calves with relaxing music on. I was sitting there just me and my thoughts. Decades ago, this would have been one way to torture me! My thoughts would have been doing the Indy 500 around my head, and my anxiety would have skyrocketed! The other day though, I just leaned back, and let it all in, stayed in the moment. That is the difference between someone trained in mindfulness and someone who was not.

I have been saying this throughout this book, but the trick for you my friend is to figure out coping skills that work for you, and what supports your mindfulness mindset. What will allow you to stay in the here and now without your thoughts becoming race cars headed for the wall on the second turn. One excellent coping skill and used in mindfulness a lot is just breathing. Taking inventory of each breath, in and out and the natural pause in between. Just sit there, eyes closed, and focus on the breath. There I gave you your first one, now what are some others?

LIVING IN THE HERE AND NOW.

REMINISCE ON SOME GOOD TIMES,
WITHOUT GETTING STUCK IN THEM.

TALK WITH FRIENDS

As the old saying goes "you can pick your friend's nose, but you can't pick your family." No, wait, that is not it, but anyway, you can pick your friends and cannot pick your family. Friends, devoted friends, are with you through thick and thin, they laugh and cry with you, sometimes both at the same time when you do something stupid. They are always there for you though, and when you need them as in times of loss, they can be one of your greatest coping skills!

I remember when I went through my Certified Peer Support Specialist training, they spoke about just being there, not saying a word, just sitting with people and being present in the moment, the here and now. That is so powerful and something we often take for granted. My friend Ryan tried to do that for me when my Uncle Vinny and Grandfather died, my depression pushed him away and I did something I knew would make him angry. I do not recommend that, although these days were back to being good friends and would drop anything to be there for each other.

Having friends and family around you in times of grief though, like I mentioned, is invaluable. Going out on the beach, to a movie, or out to eat, or just a coffee with a loyal friend is truly immeasurable.

WHO ARE YOUR LOYAL FRIENDS?

Who are your loyal friends, and why? I speak about this in my positive thinking book The Power of a Happy Mind in more detail, but why are these, loyal friends?

Stay clear of negative people and negative places!! Surround yourself with positive people, places, and those who genuinely care about you and want to help you.

A lot of us especially when younger, tend to gravitate towards the "dangerous people." People may look and act cool, or they attract us because they have stuff we want. The point is though, a lot of these people are not your true friends.

The people who are there for you in times like losing a loved one, or people who have your back, and don't give up on you no matter what. These are true friends.

When you surround yourself with positive people you will really start to feel great about yourself. People, who are your friends because they love you, not people who want something from you. Family and "true" friends will always be there. You will find out that you can count your "true" friends on one hand if you're lucky. The rest are acquaintances or people you know.

WHO ARE YOUR TRUE FRIENDS?
NOT THE 100S OF SOCIAL MEDIA FOLLOWERS,
BUT PEOPLE WHO ARE THERE FOR YOU
NO MATTER WHAT.

SUICIDE

As I am authoring this book, I am thinking of the near-death experiences I have had in my life. One rings out louder than the others, and that is my failed suicide attempt. I often talk about it as the one thing I am glad I failed in. When we are at that stage of grief, we do not think things will ever get better. We often think we have failed at life, and we do not want to go on and feel any more pain.

We do not think that things can get better (which they will). We do not think about all the lives that will be affected by ending our lives because our own pain has engulfed us in a blanket of darkness. I am speaking about that from self-experience of course. What can I also talk about from self-experience though is; what happens if we keep going?

In my talks in recovery centers and libraries on this subject I always bring up my son. My suicide attempt was over a decade ago, my son is 10yrs old, you do the math. If I succeeded in my attempt, I may have stopped my pain, but I also would have never given him a chance at life. I also would not have become an Author and an inspiration for being a survivor. I met a lot of people who blessed my life with them being in it, like the little girl I consider my daughter still to this day, or my nieces and nephews for that matter. My blessings go on and on after my attempt at never letting them in.

If you take anything away from reading this book, take away the fact that life does get better after the darkness consumes us, there is always light if we just let it in. Just take it minute by minute if you must, just keep pushing forward, reach out for help, do whatever you must to make it another day, because you never know whose life you can change, create, or inspire after you let that light in.

NEVER GIVE UP HOPE!
IF YOU FEEL LIKE YOU CAN'T GO ON, KEEP
PUSHING FORWARD, AND GET SUPPORT!

988 SUICIDE AND CRISIS LIFELINE
THE ONLY REGRET IN LIFE, IS ENDING IT PREMATURELY.

I am a U.S. Army Infantry Veteran, this year I obtained my Human Services Associates Degree, and have Certificates in Human Services & Peer Support. I also worked as a Private Investigator and Security Consultant for several years. I hold my personal experience above all else. I have had a life unlike most, I lost my parents when I was young, and some other very influential people in my life along the way. I have lived in some of the worst places as a child and I hit rock bottom over a decade ago becoming a homeless Veteran. With the VA's help I began to realize I have been living with P.T.S.D. since I was 6 years old

I eventually removed myself from the homeless situation and began to rebuild my life. I began to study martial arts Shaolin Kempo Karate and Ninjutsu to build up my self-esteem and studied grounding and mindfulness techniques, cognitive therapy, breathing techniques and mental awareness skills. As I was preparing myself for a lifelong commitment of supporting others, I came to realize that one of the most disturbing trends these days is the increase of distress across environments that were once considered safe. No safe havens exist now; we must become and provide the haven for ourselves if we are to truly cope with trauma in our lives.

For those that do not know how to create their own haven or need assistance getting out of their current abusive situations it is my hope that what I learned will help to provide long term solutions to families be it veterans or civilians that are subjected to P.T.S.D. and require help to rebuild their lives.

I still live with some trauma now and then, who does not? I only see my son on the weekends, I see his sister every other weekend, whom I still consider my daughter. Both rips a hole in my heart bigger than Texas, but I cope with it and cherish every moment with both of my children. I lost my cousin whom I idolized a couple of years back to the opioid epidemic we currently face. He was missing for 6 months, while myself, another P.I. and others searched relentlessly for him, only to be found by a hunter in the woods. The pain of losing him still cuts deep to this day, as deep as it did every day he was missing. I learned why in the Police Dept. they pull an officer away from a case if he or she gets too close to it or it involves family, because those 6 months were pure hell, only to hear someone found him and the professionals had to perform dental recognition to identify his body. I look at his picture every day and just wonder why it happened. He gives me the strength to continue doing what I do to help others like him in my community.

Cancer has taken well over a dozen people away from me in life, such as my aunt who recently passed, my uncle who raised me, and three sets of grandparents, my uncle's parents being the third. The Opioid epidemic makes my social media walls look like obituaries and I pray for my friends who still fight the battle of a lifetime constantly.

I learned the coping strategies I teach to others to help me deal with the trauma in my life be it recent or 40+ years ago, because we may be able shut the doors on our past and we may be able to block them out of our thoughts, we may even be able to take medication to ease the pain, but, to truly overcome the trauma in your lives, and in my own life, is to have long term solutions through acceptance, meditation, positive thinking, confidence building talking with someone you can trust, and other grounding techniques and coping skills; not just band-aids to cover up the wounds.

If you liked Footprints, you should check out my other publishing's and merchandise.

Website www.lifelongexperience.net

I'd really appreciate a review ☐ Reviews help author rating on amazon.com and the better rating the more people see your books. In the case of books like this one and other self-help books, the better rating the more people are supported and that's what Life Long Experience books are all about.

Go to [Review Your Purchases (amazon.com)](amazon.com) to post your honest review.

You're still here? Cool, I really hope you liked Footprints. This was the hardest book for me to write because the subject matter is my biggest stressor. I felt compelled though to get this book done, especially after we all dealt with COVID-19. With time and coping skills I brought this book to life and my hope is it brings some comfort to you after reading it, remember, you are not alone.

KEEP THEM IN YOUR HEART AND THEY'RE NEVER TRULY GONE

Dear John.

What a way to begin a letter. I always say when I lose my sense of humor, that's when we all need to worry.

This has been one of the hardest losses I've had to deal with in a while, as you were always larger than life to me. You were always the life of the party. I've been thinking a lot about losses of people larger than life, you Ricky, Leon, it's just inconceivable, but as they say nothing hits harder than life…

I want to thank you for being my life-long friend, you saved my life in so many ways man. You, Rob, Matt, Puck, Tony, Joe, Jason, Gary, when I needed a family and just didn't feel I fit in my biological one, you guys took me in, and became my brothers. You and Rob were always my ride or die, no matter what happened one thing I will never forget is when life got rough as it often did being us, we dropped whatever we had going on to be there for each other.

I'm going to tell you one thing that's been bugging me since your passing. I can tell it's been bugging me because the tears are falling as I'm writing this. I knew you were aggravated at me for pushing Rob and Matt for us to get up their which was incredibly difficult for me. I just felt it in my gut that we had very little time left. As we were walking around town that day you let me know I messed up, and I apologized, it's been on my mind though. I couldn't explain it then, that I knew if we didn't get up there when we did, we would lose our chance.

I miss ya my brother, the good times, the arguments, the brotherhood. Never in my life have I ever experienced the comradery we shared as a whole. We knew what each other were thinking before even speaking, which came in handy in bar fights. Now Rob, Puck, and Matt and I are back in each other's lives and it's great, like old times, and that's the one good thing that has come out of losing you.

People say you're gone now, but you know what I've learned, you're not. You're in my heart and in my memories.

Rest easy my brother, "we got the watch from here, while you go home."